The IRISH JOKE Book

The IRISH JOKE Book

BRENDON KELLY

Copyright © 2012 by Brendon Kelly.

ISBN: Softcover 978-1-4771-5910-1
       Ebook   978-1-4771-5911-8

All rights reserved. No part of this book may be reproduced or transmitted in any form or by any means, electronic or mechanical, including photocopying, recording, or by any information storage and retrieval system, without permission in writing from the copyright owner.

To order additional copies of this book, contact:
Xlibris Corporation
0800-891-366
www.xlibris.co.nz
Orders@Xlibris.co.nz
700313

THE IRISH JOKE BOOK

What is five miles long, green and has an IQ of 25?

A St. Patrick Day's march.

What has an IQ of 15 and digs holes in the road?

15 Irish laborers.

What has an IQ of 19 and digs holes in the road?

A wombat.

What is written on the bottom of Irish beer bottles?

"Open other end".

What is written on the top of Irish beer bottles?

"See other end for instructions".

Why do Irish dogs have flat faces?

They chase parked cars.

How do you burn an Irishman's ear?

Phone him while he is ironing.

How did the Irishman burn his other ear?

He had to ring the doctor didn't he.

How did the Irishman drown?

He was trying to push start a submarine.

How do you sink an Irish submarine?

Knock on the hatch.

What do you do if an Irishman throws a pin at you?

Run. He has probably got a grenade in his mouth.

What do you do if an Irishman throws a grenade at you?

Pull the pin out and throw it back.

What is black and crisp and hangs from the ceiling?

An Irish electrician.

How many Irishmen does it take to make popcorn?

Five. One to hold the pan and four to shake the stove.

How many Irishmen does it take to paint a house?

3,000. One to hold the paint brush and 2,999 to move the house up and down.

Why does it take ten Irishmen to change a lightbulb?

One to hold the lightbulb and nine to turn the ladder.

What's the difference between a ham sandwich and an Irishman?

A ham sandwich is only half an inch thick.

What's the difference between an Irishman and a100 ham sandwiches?

Nothing.

Did you hear about the Irishman who was sent to London to blow up a bus?

He burnt his lips on the exhaust.

What's an Irish four-course meal?

Baked potato, boiled potato, mashed potato and chips.

How do you make an Irishman dizzy?

Put him in a barrel and tell him to go sit in the corner.

An Irishman walked into a hospital with a large hole where his armpit should be. The doctor said, "You're the fifth person to present with these symptoms this week. How did this happen?"

"Well doctor," replied the Irishman. "I pulled the pin out of my hand grenade and started counting." The Irishman counts on his fingers. "One, two, three, four, five." He tucks hand grenade under arm to use other hand. "Six, seven, eight, boom."

An Irishman was digging a hole when his friend approached.

"What are you doing?" asked his friend.

"I'm digging a hole to bury my dog," replied the intrepid excavator.

"Well, what are these other three holes for?" persisted the friend.

"They were going to be to bury my dog in but they weren't big enough," explained the Irishman.

Did you hear about the Irishman who wanted to tap-dance.

He broke his ankle when he fell off the sink.

Did you hear about the Irishman who was given some water skis?

He spent the rest of his life looking for a sloping lake.

Did you hear about the Irish water polo team?

They drowned four horses at their first trial.

This Irishman was walking home from a fair carrying a pig under his arm, and a guy who knew him came up to him and asked him, "Where did you get that?"

The pig spoke up and said, "I won him at the fair."

Why do Irishmen hang around in groups of three?

One can usually read, one can usually write, and the other one likes to hang around with intellectuals.

Why don't the Irish fly planes?

Because they are still learning to walk.

Aer Lingus pilot with plane in trouble radios, "Mayday, mayday, mayday."

Air Traffic Controls responds, "You are cleared to land. Can you give us your height and position?"

The pilot says, "Well, I'm five foot eight and sitting in the cockpit."

Why was Jesus born in Jerusalem instead of Dublin?

Because there weren't three wise men or a virgin in Dublin.

How do you make an Irishman laugh on a Monday?

Tell him a joke on a Friday.

Do you hear the joke about the Irish marksman who shot an arrow at the air and missed . . . ?

His brother was the Irish champion parachutist.

He jumped out of a plane and missed the earth.

Boss to new bus driver, "Tomorrow you start on the one-man buses. You do both jobs—collect fares and drive."

Next day—fearful accident in town. Bus hits building. Turns out the driver was upstairs collecting fares at the time of the crash.

What do you call a man with his hand up an Irishman's bum?

A brain surgeon.

Two Irishmen driving to a pub with a bomb in the back and evil plans in mind. One of them says, "What if the bomb goes off before we get there?"

The other replies, "Don't worry, I have a spare bomb in the boot."

Paddy thinks that his turn indicator isn't working, so he asks Sean to run along behind him and see. Sean calls out, "It's working . . . now it's not . . . now it's working . . . now it's not . . ."

Why is the suicide rate low among Irishmen?

It's pretty hard to kill yourself jumping out of basement windows.

What do you call an Irishman with half a brain?

Lucky.

What do you call an Irishman with a degree?

A damned liar.

How can you pick an Irishman pirate?

He wears an eye patch over both eyes.

Not all Irishman are totally dumb. After all it was an Irishman who invented an ejector seat for helicopters.

Did you hear about the Irishman who tried to take his new car for its first service?

It wouldn't fit through the church doors.

Did you hear about the Irish space mission that failed?

Their rubber band broke.

Why is it that the windows on the bottom floors of Irish apartment buildings are always dirty?

They can't dig a hole deep enough to fit the ladder in.

Why do Irish council workers have tea breaks that are only ten minutes long?

Because if they wait any longer they have to be retrained.

Two Irishmen decide to rob a Sydney bank. During the robbery they decide not to say anything for fear their accents will give them away. They thought of writing the hold-up note, but neither of them could write. Finally they hired a speech therapist to teach them the subtle intonations of the Sydney accent. After the lesson, they entered the bank, pointed their shotguns at the teller and said, "Allrightmategiveusallyourmoneyorwe'llblowyourbloodyeadorf."

The teller looked up and said calmly, "You're Irish aren't you?"

Stunned they could only stammer, "B-b-but, h-how did you know? Our accents were perfect."

The teller replied, "You've sawn your shotguns off at the wrong end."

Why did the Irish stop making ice blocks?

Because the old lady who knew the recipe died.

Why are the Irish toilet rolls 500 sheets longer?

Because the first 500 sheets are instructions.

It was a rip-roaring Shamus O'Grady who came to London expecting to find it paved with gold and instead found it thick with coppers.

Why do the Arabs have oil and the Irish have potatoes?

Because the Irish had first choice.

How do you keep an Irishman busy all day?

Give him a piece of paper with P.T.O written on both sides of sheet.

There was an Irishman walking down the street with a sack over his shoulder. A friend came up to him and said, "What's in the bag Mick?" Mick replied, "Chickens, Pat. And I'll tell you what. If you can guess how many I've got I'll give you both of them.

Pat answered, "Three."

A man walks into a bar and said to the bartender, "I've got some great Irish jokes for you."

The bartender replied, "Yeah, well I'm Irish—don't worry."

"I'll say them slowly," said the Irishman.

Paddy and Sean are driving through Dublin when a loud bang is heard from below. Sean gets out to see what's wrong, and says to Paddy, "Your tire is flat. But you can still drive on it—only the bottom part is flat."

Because of their recently acquired wealth, the Arabs decided that they had to hold an international sports tournament. So they decided to hold a domino tournament. They invited contestants from everywhere including Ireland. The tournament progressed very well, and just before getting eliminated, the Irishman noticed that the dots on the dominos were actually diamonds.

He thought that they wouldn't miss one. So in his last game he slipped one into his shoe. No-one noticed and he quickly left to catch Aer Lingus home. He didn't take it out of his shoe, just in case someone saw him. He got himself home as quickly as he could, considering he had to limp. He bolted all the doors and took off his shoe. He could hardly contain himself, thinking about his new found wealth. He took the domino out and turned it over—double-blank.

Did you ever hear about this Irishman who had these two horses that he couldn't tell apart? He always had lots of trouble until one day he discovered that the white horse was two hands taller than the black horse.

Do you know why the Irish haven't launched a spaceship, even though the Americans and the Russians have launched them for years?

They haven't as yet found a bottle large enough for the stick.

How do you recognize an Irish skin-diver?

He has water-wings.

How can you keep a hungry Irishman busy for months?

Give him a bag of crisps with "Open Each End" on both ends of the packet.

What's the difference between a disaster and a catastrophe?

A disaster is when a ship full of 1000 Irishmen sinks. A catastrophe is when all of them can swim.

One day two Irishman were walking in the woods when they came across a sign saying "Tree fellers wanted".

One of them said, "You know, Sean, it's a shame Paddy isn't with us today. We could have gotten a job."

Do you realise that many Australians are of Irish descent? I mean, think of your closest friends. How often do have to explain Irish jokes to them several times?

How many Irishman does it take to drain a field?

2000 to lift the field and 500 to dig sand under it.

How does an Irishman catch flies?

He carries them up to the hayloft and then kicks away the ladder.

Why are Irishman always buried in coffins with only two handles?

Have you ever seen a garbage can with four handles?

How does an Irishman catch mice?

He chases them under a table and quickly saws of its legs.

What's so special when an Irishman swallows a fly?

Well, he's got more brains in his stomach than in his head.

What has an Irishman got inside his skull?

A piece of paper saying "brain" on it.

How many Irishman does it take to milk a cow?

24. Four to hold on to its udder and the rest to lift the cow up and down.

Why do Irishmen take a stone and a box of matches to bed?

They put out the light with the stone then they light a match to check if it is really out.

Why can't one put an Irishman in a cannon?

Because according to the Geneva convention dum-dum bullets are illegal.

How many Irishman does it take to hit a nail into a wall?

22. One to hold the hammer, 1 to hold the nail and 20 to shove the wall forward.

Heard about the latest innovation in Irish submarines?

Screen windows to keep the fish out.

Why is it difficult for the Irish to become magicians?

An Irish magician, holding both hands out in front of him, one closed the other opened says, "In one of my hands, I have a pea. Now which one . . ."

Did you hear about the Irish Godfather who was given an offer he could not remember?

An Irishman was walking down the street with one glove on one hand.

A guy walked up to him and asked, "Why do you only have one glove on?"

"Well," replied the Irishman, "the weather announcer said that it would be cold today but on the other hand it was going to be warm."

What has an IQ of 180?

Ireland.

There were two Santa's coming down the chimney, which one was Irish?

The one with a bag of Easter eggs.

What is the definition of gross ignorance?

144 Irishmen.

What is the fastest game in the world?

Pass the parcel in an Irish pub.

How is an Irish ladder different to an ordinary one?

It has a Stop sign at the top.

Why did the bald Irishman paint bunnies on his head?

Because from a distance he thought they would look like hares.

Irishman—"How am I going to measure this pole?"

Friend—"Lay it on its side and pace it out."

Irishman—"I want to measure its height not its length."

What's the definition of a dope ring?

Six Irishman in a circle.

The scene—Building a new house in Ireland. A foreman comes over to the workman who says, "These nails won't go in the wood."

"Of course not," the foreman replies, "you're hammering them in head first. These nails go in the other side of the house."

Did you hear about the new Irish parachute?

It opens on impact.

Did you see the party where all the Irishmen were on the roof?

They had heard that the drinks were on the house.

Did you hear about the Irish doctor who invented an appendix transplant?

An Irishman walked into a pub with a big green bullfrog on his head.

The barman asked, "Where did you get that from?"

The bullfrog said, "Would you believe it started as a wart on my behind."

A Scotsman wanted to have an operation to change into an Australian. The operation consisted of removing 20% of his brain and leaving eighty percent. After the operation the surgeon apologized to the patient for making a mistake. He'd removed 80% of his brain and left only twenty percent.

"Ah, it's grand," replied the patient.

Did you hear about the Irishman who sued the local baker for forging his signature on a hot cross bun?

Did you hear about the Irishman who broke his leg raking leaves?

He fell out of the tree.

An Irishwoman was complaining about her oral contraceptive. She said for all the good it did her she may as well have swallowed it.

On the sporting scene, the first national Irish steeplechase was cancelled. Not one horse could get a grip on the cathedral roof.

A big Irishman called Paddy saunters into a Dublin bar and shouts, "Which one of you is Michael O' Shea?"

"I am," replies a short Irishman from a corner.

Paddy walks over to him and punches him in the mouth.

THE IRISH JOKE BOOK

The little fellow starts laughing so Paddy hits him again and he falls down, still laughing. He staggers to his feet still laughing. Paddy can't bear it, and shouts, "Why are you laughing after I've belted you?"

The little man says, "The jokes on you. I'm not Michael O'Shea."

What do you call a pregnant Irishwoman?

A dope carrier.

Did you hear about the Irishman who was in a duel and came third.

One day Sean was walking his dog down the street. When they neared a man reading a newspaper, the dog cocked his leg and wet the man's trousers. The man was understandably upset and exclaimed, "Can't you teach your dog to do his business in the gutter?"

The next day Sean was walking down the street when he came across the same man.

"Where's your dog?" asked the man.

"He's dead," replied Sean. "I was teaching him to do his business in the gutter like you said when he fell off the roof."

Did you hear about the Irishwoman ironing her curtains?

She fell out of the window.

Paddy was telling Sean about the fantastic soccer match he was at the other day. Sean was very interested and excitedly asked him what the score was. Paddy said that it was nil all, and then went on to describe some of the more exciting things that happened in the game. Sean, getting more interested, asked him what the score was at half-time. Paddy said that he didn't know as he only arrived in the second half.

Paddy didn't think much of sex on the TV. He kept falling off.

Irishman on the telephone says, "Well if you're the wrong number, then why did you answer the phone?"

An Irish woman was explaining to her doctor how she got a headache applying cosmetics. She was applying toilet water to her neck when the toilet seat fell on her head.

How would you recognize an aircraft designed by an Irishman?

By the outside toilets.

Twelve jurors had just been appointed for a court case in Ireland.

"Gentlemen of the jury," said the clerk of the court. "You should proceed to your accustomed places."

The court erupted in confusion when the Irishmen clambered to fit into the dock.

An Irishman saw a lobster pot for the first time and, having been told what it was called, said, "I find it very hard to believe that you could get any lobster to sit on one of those things."

Did you hear about the Irishman who thought that aperitif was French for a set of dentures?

An Irish lawyer was representing a man who was charged with murdering his parents by chopping their heads off with an axe. The defence counsel opened by saying, "Ladies and gentlemen of the jury, consider this poor orphan . . ."

How does an Irishman choose the spot in a Spot the Ball competition?

He takes a pin and pushes it into the picture until he hears a pssst.

How many Irishmen does it take to carry out a kidnapping?

Ten. One to do the kidnapping and nine to write the ransom note.

Did you hear about the Irish hemophiliac who died trying a new form of treatment?

Acupuncture.

How do you recognize an Irish cuckoo clock?

Each twenty-five minutes the cuckoo pops out and asks the time.

How do you sink a submarine designed by an Irishman?

Put it in water.

An Irishman joined the army and after three years was awarded the special crossed knife and fork insignia. He had achieved the distinction of three years of eating with a knife and fork without incident.

An Irish traffic warden explained the system of yellow parking lines on Dublin roads. "One yellow line means no parking at all, and two yellow lines means no parking at all at all."

Mick, who had been working in England, went back to Ireland to find that his mates, Lenny and Sean were going to Liverpool for the first time.

"You'll love England," he said, "Everything's so big there. The money's big, the birds are big, the buildings are big, and the building sites—wow!"

Lenny and Sean arrived in Liverpool and as they walked down the gangplank, Sean saw an anchor on the pier. "Begorrah Lenny, Mick wasn't kidding. Look at the size of dat pickaxe over dere."

A magistrate was giving judgment. "Young man," he said sternly, "It is alcohol, and alcohol alone that is responsible for your appearance before this bench."

"I'm very glad you think that," said the young man. "Me mam says it's me own fault."

Two very drunk Englishmen were arguing about whether the shiny object in the sky was the sun or the moon. An Irishman happened to be passing by, one of the Englishmen said to him, "I say sir, is that the sun or the moon up there?"

"I don't know," said the Irishman. "I'm a stranger around here."

O'Reilly was a bit maudlin and turned to his best friend and said, "I'd like you to promise me Sean, that when I'm dead and buried, that you'll pour a bottle of the best Irish whiskey over my grave."

"I'll do that for you," said his friend, "but would you have any objections if it passed through my kidneys first?"

"I always like to go to Paddy's birthday party and help him drink his presents," said an Irishman to his friend.

"I don't really drink myself," said the other Irishman, "I gargle it, but sometimes it slips down."

The magistrate looked sternly down at the offender in the dock.

"Why did you kick and punch this woman so brutally?" he asked.

"Sure, and it was an honest mistake, your Honour," said the offender. "I had had a few drinks and was confused. I thought it was my wife."

One of Sean's friends asked him why he no longer wore glasses.

"I read so much about the evils of drinking," he replied. "Either I had to give up drinking, or give up reading."

An Irishman, noted for his tall stories, was telling a tourist about how hot it was last summer. "Why, I saw a fox being chased by hounds one day," he said, "and it was so hot they were all walking."

How do you recognize an Irish pencil?

It got an eraser at both ends.

Two Irishmen were wrestling with a piano at the top of the stairs.

"It's no good," said one, "we'll never get this upstairs."

"Upstairs?" said the other, "I thought we were trying to take it down."

An Irishman went to the Post Office for six stamps. He'd had six letters from his friend and he thought he'd better answer them.

The Irish paratroop trainees were flying out for their first parachute jump after completing training.

"Remember lads. Yell Geronimo, jump out, count to ten and then pull your ripcord."

The plane leveled out at 10,000 feet and the door opened. All the lads jumped out and Paddy went last. The instructor shut the door and the plane flew down and landed. When he got out the instructor saw Paddy desperately clinging to the wing of the plane.

"What the hell happened to you?" yelled the instructor.

"Sorry sir," stammered Paddy, "but I forgot the name of that Indian I was supposed to yell when I jumped out of the plane."

An old Irishman went for a well-deserved holiday on the west coast of Ireland for the sake of his health. He stayed in a lovely bed and breakfast near the sea, took daily walks and enjoyed his restful break. He hadn't been back two days when he died. Two of his friends came to the wake and were standing in the front room looking at him lying peacefully in the open coffin.

"Doesn't he look wonderful?" asked one.

"He does look grand," said the other. "That long holiday on the coast must've done him the world of good."

Two Texans went into a Dublin pub.

"A pint of ya best Guinness," barked the burly Texan. "And buddy, make sure the glass is clean."

The barman poured the two pints in the usual way, letting them sit before finishing them off.

"Come on buddy. What's the hold up?" asked the other Texan.

The barman pulled the handle down to finish each pint right to the very top, one after the other.

He took a step back and announced, "Two pints of Guinness. And which one of you asked for the clean glass?"

The Irish space program has again run into difficulties. The astronaut keeps falling of the kite.

How do you make an Irish martini?

Put one potato into a pint of Guinness.

A gorilla escaped from the zoo and adopted an Irishman. One day they were out for a walk. A policeman went over to the Irishman.

"What's going on here sir?" asked the policeman.

"I don't know," said the Irishman, "This big monkey just found me and took me by the hand."

"Well," said the policeman. "You'd better take that gorilla to the zoo."

The Irishman agreed and wandered off with the gorilla, still holding his hand.

Next day the policeman was making his rounds when he was shocked to see the same Irishman holding the gorilla by the hand. "Hey," shouted the policeman, "I thought it told you yesterday to take that gorilla to the zoo."

"I did," said the Irishman, "and he liked it so much we're just going again."

An Irishman travelling through a remote part of Yorkshire found the pace of life even more leisurely than similar places in Ireland.

"Will you tell me," he says to a Yorkshireman, "why is it that you people take life so easy?"

"Well," replied the Yorkshireman, "around these parts we have a saying, 'Never do today what you can put off 'til tomorrow'."

"We have a similar attitude back where I come from," says the Irishman, "but we don't have the same sense of urgency."

Pat was dawdling on his way to work. As Mick walked past him, he saw that he was half-asleep and slapped him on the back.

"Morning' Pat," said Mick, "It's half asleep you're lookin'."

Pat turned a bleary eye on his friend. "And it's half asleep I'm feelin'," said Pat. "Wasn't I up half the night."

"If you don't mind me askin'," says Mick, "what was the trouble?"

"I was worried about the cat," says Pat, "I was awake until 2 waiting for him to come in, so I could let him out for the night."

It was a stormy night in County Mayo when farmer Sean rang the doctor to come as his wife's waters had broke.

As the doctor was preparing to deliver the baby, a bolt of lightning put the power out. Sean found a large torch and held it while the doctor delivered the baby.

"Sean, you're the proud father of a little boy," said the doctor.

"Grand," said Sean, "I'll fetch a glass each so we can celebrate."

"Just wait," said the doctor, "will ye hold the torch a little closer, I think there's another one coming. Yes, you're the proud father of two boys," said the doctor.

"Well isn't that something," said Sean. "Two o' 'dem. I fetch the bottle then."

"One more moment," exclaimed the doctor, "hold the light closer. I think there's another one."

"Begorrah," says Sean, "I don't want to be conclusive, but do you think the light's attracting 'em."

Mick and Paddy were commiserating over Sean's recent death. When the pub called last drinks they decided to go and see him. Staggering down the main street they eventually came across the funeral parlor. Forcing the back door, they went in and bumbled about in the dark until one fell over a piano and banged his head on the floor.

"Here's the coffin Paddy," said Mick, as he got up rubbing his head.

"Did you recognize him?" asked Paddy.

"No," admitted Mick, "But he had a fine set of teeth, to be sure."

The Irish priest glowered down over the congregation from the pulpit. He was one of those fire-and-brimstone priests whose thunderous sermons put the fear of God into the congregation every Sunday. Today the priest was bellowing about the demon drink.

"Drink!" shouted the priest. "It is the greatest curse of the country. It makes yer quarrel with your neighbours. It makes yer spend all yer rent money. It makes yer shoot at yer landlord—and it makes yer miss!"

THE IRISH JOKE BOOK

During a long Atlantic crossing, an old Jew called Di and an Irishman called Mick argued every day about what happened what death struck. During the journey, the old Jew fell ill and died. The crew gave him a dignified burial at sea with the body bag weighed down with coal.

"Well Sean," said Mick to his friend, "maybe Di knew the day was coming sooner than he thought. But I'll wager the heathen never dreamed he'd have to take his own fuel."

Mrs. O'Sullivan wanted her son to go on an errand for her. "Sean," said Mrs. O' Sullivan, "would you ever go down to the butcher's for our lunch. Fetch four o' dose sausages hanging up in the window."

"Sure Ma," said Sean, and off he went. Hours passed and eventually Sean came home empty handed.

"I couldn't find the sausages like you said Ma. All the sausages were hanging down."

"Paddy, do you understand French?"

"Yes, if it's spoken in Oirish."

Sean was at the horse races, and he had his eye on a particular horse. He decided to place a bet on it and approached a bookmaker he knew. He bet $1 on the horse and was amazed when it paid $1000 when it won at odds of 1000 to 1. Sean went back to the bookmaker to collect his winnings.

"I'm sorry Sean," said the bookmaker. "You've caught me a little short at the moment as I didn't expect that nag to come in at all. But I can pay you in a few days time."

"But I want me money now," pleaded Sean.

"Well, 'cos I don't have the cash," said the bookmaker, "would you accept a bank check?"

"I bet with you in cash," Sean said, "and cash is what I'm wanting to be paid in. If it'll help I'll make the odds 500 to 1."

"No I'm sorry," said the bookie, "I just don't have that much."

"How about 250 to 1," said Sean.

"No, I really can't pay you cash today," insisted the bookie.

"Well, if that's the way it is," said the frustrated Irishman, "the bet's off."

Two Irishmen were walking along the beach. One said to the other, "Hey, did you see that dead seagull?"

The other one looked skyward and said, "No, where?"

I suppose most of us have heard of Murphy's Law of Maximum Inconvenience. If we had we would have been amazed at its theoretical and practical implications. For example, if there is a 50-50 chance of something happening the way that would suit you, the odds are four to one against you, or when you drop something it will roll underneath the bench where you are working. It's interesting to ponder on the fact that Murphy is an Irish name.

Two Irishmen were walking past an English pub just after an IRA bomb explosion. They spotted a blood-covered Irish comrade lying dead face-down on the pavement.

One of them grabbed the collar of the dead man and dragged him up so he might see who he was.

"Isn't that Patrick Donovan?" asked his friend.

"No. It's too tall to be Patrick."

A chronic alcoholic had an appointment with a specialist in Dublin hospital. The doctor told the patient that he had to have a brain transplant.

"Good news," said the doctor," we have a brain bank where you can choose your new brain."

"However," continued the doctor, "the bad news is that because of heavy demand, there are only three brains left."

"We have this brain from an Australian valued at $1500," he said. "Or you could have a brain from a German engineer for twice that, or finally we have an Irish brain."

"Well doctor," said the Irishman, "I'd like the Irish brain, of course."

"I suppose you would," said the doctor, "but I must warn you. It's $10,000."

"Begorrah," said the Irishman, "That's a lot. Why is it so much?"

"It's never been used," said the doctor.

An Indian, a Jew and an Irishman happened to be travelling together through the Irish countryside when it got dark and they decided to find somewhere to spend the night.

They saw a light on at a farmhouse and stopped to ask if they could stay the night.

"Well, okay," said the farmer, "but there's only room for two in the house. One of you will have to sleep in the barn."

"I'll use the barn then," volunteered the Indian with a shake of the head.

Not ten minutes had gone by when he knocked on the door of the farmhouse.

"I cannot sleep in the barn as there is a sacred cow there, so I cannot."

"All-right then, I'll go into the barn, "said the Jew.

Not ten minutes had gone by when the Jew knocked on the door of the house.

"There is a pig in the barn. I will not tolerate being in such close proximity to such an animal," said the Jew.

"Ah well," said the Irishman, "I'll be going out there then."

So the Irishman walked out to the barn.

Not ten minutes had gone by but the farmer hears a knock on the door of the house.

When the farmer went to the door and opened it, there stood the cow and the pig.

A building site was in desperate need of another worker.

At a job interview, the foreman held up his left hand. "Which hand is this?" he asked the job applicant.

"Ah . . . er . . . um," hesitated the Irishman.

"L . . . l," prompted the foreman.

THE IRISH JOKE BOOK

"Left," answered the Irishman.

The foreman then held up his other hand. "Which hand is this?" he asked,

"Ah . . . er . . . um," stumbled the Irishman.

"It starts with 'R'," said the foremen.

"R . . . well that'd be the right," said the Irishman.

The Irishman was given the job and arrived first thing the following morning. It was a freezing cold morning and he arrived to find the foreman rubbing his hands together trying to get them warm.

"Now, you're just trying to confuse me," said the Irishman.

This is the story of how an Irish bricklayer's laborer brought down a load of extra bricks from the top of the scaffolding built for the job.

The Irishman devised a method, using a hod to pile the bricks on, a rope and a pulley. He would load the hod with bricks, climb down to the ground, pull on the rope so that the hod would swing clear of the scaffold planks, and slowly let it down by paying out the rope.

Unfortunately, the Irishman put far too many bricks on the hod so that it was heavier than him.

Once freed at the top, its weight started to pull him up on the rope.

As they passed the hod crashed into his shoulder.

The hod continued down, he continued up. Because he was holding the rope, his fingers were crushed as they passed under the pulley. At about this time, the hod hit the ground with a jolt, which dislodged most of the bricks. Now the Irishman was heavier than the hod. So the Irishman began to fall, pulling the hod up. When they passed the second time, the hod crashed against his legs. The Irishman continued down until he fell heavily arse-first on the jumbled pile of bricks. With crushed fingers, a sore shoulder, butt and legs the Irishman was amazed that he wasn't dead. Such was his surprise that he let go of the rope, causing the hod to fall and crash on his head.

When the dust cleared, the Irishman lifted himself up onto his haunches and asked if he was eligible for sick leave.

Did you hear about the Irishman who became very conscious of personal hygiene?

He decided to put on fresh socks every day. By the end of the week he couldn't get his shoes on.

An Irishman went to the office in a yard to be interviewed for a job as a bricklayer. He was told by the foreman that he must answer three questions correctly.

"How many bricks in that wall over there?" asked the foreman.

"15500," said the Irishman.

"Lucky guess," said the foreman, "and correct. "Second question—How many bags of cement in a ton?"

"Twenty," replied the Irishman.

"Right," said the foreman. "Third question, where was Jesus born?"

"I don't know the answer to that one," said the Irishman.

"Well, you'd better find out. And let me know when you do," said the foreman.

THE IRISH JOKE BOOK

So the Irishman walked out of the office and across the yard. Before he left he noticed some workmen milling about and decided to see if they knew the answer to the third question.

"Jesus was born in Bethlehem," answered one of the workmen.

"Beth . . . Beth . . . I don't think I'll be able to remember that," said the Irishman. "Would you write it down for me?"

"Here," said the workman. "I'll write it on this brick."

He wrote on the brick and handed it to the Irishman. Off went the happy Irishman back to the office to see the foreman. "I've found out where Jesus was born." The Irishman reads off the brick. "BEN TULLEY".

Do you know the difference between baloney and blarney?

To tell a woman of forty-five that she looks like a young girl is baloney.

To ask her how old she is so that you'll know at what age a woman looks her best is blarney.

An Irishman's mother-in-law passed away and his wife asked him what sort of gravestone they should get her mother.

"Something very, very heavy," he replied.

A very tall man wearing a cowboy hat was on an Aer Lingus flight to Shannon in Ireland.

When she reached him the stewardess asked, "Can I get you a drink, sir?"

"Yeah sure," the American said in a loud voice so everyone around could hear. "A whiskey. By the way, I'm from Texas, I'm white from the top of my six foot six inches to the tip of my toes and I hate the Irish. My name's Brown, that's spelt B-R-O-W-N."

The stewardess poured his drink, gave it to him and moved down the aisle.

The man sitting next to the Texan turned to him and said, "How do you do? My name is O'Reilley, and I'm from Dublin. I'm white from the top of my five foot eight inches to the tip of my toes apart for my arse, which is brown. That's spelt B-R-O-W-N."

A priest was giving his parishioners his usual sermon.

"Abstinence," he said, "is a wonderful thing, to be sure, a wonderful thing."

Unusually, a voice came from the back of the congregation. "Sure and I know it is Father," a man's voice called, "if practiced in moderation."

Paddy and Mick were at the local drinking Guinness. The craic turned to the English.

"It's not true that the English are against us," said Paddy. "If you go to London and you meet an Englishman, he'll probably take you home; he may even share his bed with you, and give you breakfast in the morning. All for free."

"Very friendly all-together," said Mick. "Did that happen to you then Paddy?"

"No," said Paddy. "But it happened to my sister."

Sean was out digging in the garden one day when he saw a weird creature at his feet and he lifted up his shovel to kill it.

To his surprise, the creature spoke. "Wait," it shouted, "spare my life and I'll grant you three wishes. I'm a leprechaun."

"Three wishes. Done," said Sean. "Well, I'm thirsty from all of this digging, so I'd like a bottle of cold Guinness."

The leprechaun snapped his fingers, and Sean found himself holding an ice-cold bottle of Guinness.

"Dat dere," said the leprechaun, "is a magic bottle. It'll never empty. It'll pour forever."

Sean tipped the cold Guinness down his throat, and gulped once, twice, three times. As he righted the bottle, it was refilled immediately.

"What are your next two wishes?" asked the leprechaun.

Sean pointed to the bottle. "Gimme two more o' dose."

Did you hear the sad story of the Irish woodworm?

It was found dead in a brick.

Did you hear about the Irish good-time-girl who was at a serious disadvantage because she couldn't spell?

She didn't make any money in her first month because she kept turning up at the warehouse.

The Irish once more entered the space race. They designed and built a space capsule and launch rocket. The space capsule was only large enough for a man and possibly a small child. So instead of a small child they decided to use a monkey. The Irishman and the monkey were duly chosen as the astronauts, trained, given their sealed instructions and launched. Having reached full speed with the final rocket stage being jettisoned, it was time to open their instructions. The monkey opened his envelope first. His multi-page instructions were headed Telemetry Controls, Orbital Adjustments, and Re-entry Procedures etc.

Having glanced at the monkey's instructions, the Irishman eagerly ripped open his envelope to find only one sheet of paper. It said, "Don't forget to feed the monkey."

Pat and Mick decided to go fishing. They went to the boat hire shop where they made the cheapest deal they could, hired a boat and all the fishing gear they needed. They rowed out to the center of the lake; they pulled the oars in and decided to have a try to catch a fish.

"Faith and begorrah," said Pat, "this be such a fine thing to do. Why don't we do this again t'morra Mick?"

"That'd be a grand idea," said Mick.

After a long pause Mick said, "How do we find this good place again?"

"That's easy," said Pat, "we'll put a mark on the side of the boat."

"But Pat," said Mick, "how do you know we'll get the same boat again?"

A business executive of a multi-national company in London was suffering from the pressures of work. He felt stressed, run down and tired. He realised that he was depressed and felt so overwhelmed that he thought he might be going to have a mental breakdown. He was referred to a psychiatrist who referred him to a neurologist. The Harley Street neurologist told the executive about a new procedure that was analogous to an engine overhaul that had remarkable success. It involved removing the brain and giving it a complete clean and overhaul. The operation went without a hitch.

A month passed and the rejuvenated brain sat in a large pitcher of clear liquid being kept alive by a machine. The business executive had not been back to collect it. The neurologist had tried the executive's direct dial, but to no avail. He decided to phone the company head office in New York and left a message with Human Resources for them to get back to him.

Eventually an email arrived which said, "Brain no longer required. Transferred to Dublin branch."

Two Irishmen were talking in a Dublin pub.

"I wouldn't go to America if you paid me," said Jerry.

"Why not?" said Stephen.

"Well for one thing, you drive on the right-hand side of the road," said Jerry.

"And, what's wrong with that?" asked Stephen.

"Well I tried it the other day when I drove to Galway, and it was just terrible," said Jerry.

Did you hear about the Irishman who thought a V8 Rover was a bionic dog?

Paddy and Mick, his co-pilot, are about to land an Aer Lingus Airbus for the first time at a new airport. They had just passed over the airport perimeter fence when Paddy said, "This runway appears to be very short."

Just as the wheels touched, Paddy applied the brakes, full reverse thrust and full flaps to bring the plane to a screaming halt with its wheels almost touching the grass.

"Hell," exclaimed Paddy, "that's the shortest runway I've ever landed on."

"Yeah," said Mick, as he looked from side-to-side out of the cockpit, "and one of the widest too."

After aircraft maintenance had replaced the tires, the same pilots were scheduled to fly on the first Aer Lingus flight to Moscow. They were looking forward to spending the night in a hotel that had been booked for them just beside the Kremlin. They landed on the long runway and the hotel collected them in a limo. They were directed to their room—a lavish suite on the first floor of the hotel.

"Mick," said Paddy, "what if the room has been bugged?"

"Do you think so?" asked Mick.

"I wouldn't put it past them," replied Paddy.

So the two pilots searched for listening devices. They searched for hours, but the only sign of a bug was a slight bulge in the carpet. Using hand signals, and writing notes to each other, the two men managed to lift the carpet and found a convex metal disc screwed to the floor.

Using Mick's trusty penknife, the men undid the screws. Just as the last screw was being removed, a massive crash could be heard from the floor below. The chandelier in the foyer had shattered on the foyer floor.

An Irishman was taking part in a quiz contest for a $10,000 prize.

"And now for $10,000, Patrick" said the compere, "what are the first names of these famous statesmen who died by assassination? Remember," reiterated the compere, "you have thirty seconds to answer."

"Yes", said Patrick.

"All-right then," said the compere in a voice laced with tension. "For ten thousand dollars, what are the first names of these men: Kennedy, King and Gandhi?"

Patrick looked down at the floor as the music swelled.

"Ten seconds . . ." said the compere.

"I'm afraid you might've beaten me with the first two," said Patrick, "but was the third Goosey Goosey?"

Two Irishmen were talking about a friend.

"Poor Mick. Poor Mick is dead," said Sean.

"I didn't know that," said Trent. "How did he die?"

"He died when a train ran over his finger," replied Sean.

"How could he die just because a train ran over his finger?" asked Trent.

"Well," said Sean, "he was picking his nose at the time."

An Irish farmer walked up to his friend holding out a huge pile of fresh horse manure in his hand, and said, "Look what I nearly stepped in."

What is 30 feet long and gives the greatest of pleasure?

A busload of Irishmen going over a cliff.

What do you get when you cross an Irishman with an ape?

A retarded ape.

What do you call an Irishman who marries a pig?

A social climber.

Where is the safest place in Ireland to hide a five pound note?

Under a bar of soap.

How do you know when an Irishman has been in your pool?

There's a ring around it.

What did the Irishman say to his wife when he came back from the unemployment office?

"Good news, dear. I got you a job."

What is a fire in a garbage bin?

An Irish barbeque.

What is the best-selling book in Ireland?

1001 Wife-beating Methods.

What do you get for throwing petrol bombs in Ireland?

About 20 Protestants per gallon.

Why did the Irish kamikaze pilots only fly one mission?

Because they never had the guts to fly a second.

What is the definition of air pollution?

1000 Irish paratroopers.

How do you keep Irishmen out of your backyard?

Keep your garbage bins in the front.

How is the census conducted in Ireland?

They count the number of basement windows and multiply by fifty.

How do you tell the difference between an English sewer and an Irish sewer?

Irish sewers have diving boards.

What is harder than selling ice to Eskimos?

Selling soap to Irishmen.

What second-hand item is hard to come by in Ireland?

A used bath.

Why are there no Irish tradesmen?

None has lived long enough to complete apprenticeship.

An amateur Irish aviator was lost after having been blown off course by very strong winds. The only radio contact he could make advised him to fly into London airport, on a particular bearing.

BBC News: "Measures are now underway for an emergency at London airport. Official sources could not give any reason for what seems to be a kamikaze-like attack . . ."

How do you brainwash an Irishman?

Fill his boots with water.

How do you recognize an Irish tank?

It has one forward gear and nine reverse gears. The forward gear is in case of rear attack.

On hearing of an Irish mother who had thirty children, the Pope sent a Cardinal to congratulate her on her achievement. He found his way to her house in the back streets of Dublin and knocked on the door. The lady of the house answered the door and the Cardinal cleared his throat and delivered his message, "I'm here to congratulate you on having thirty children. The Pope is very proud of you," he said.

"I'm a Protestant," said the woman. "But thanks anyway."

"Are you really?" asked the Cardinal.

"Indeed I am," replied the woman.

"You . . . you total sex maniac," said the Cardinal.

Paddy told everyone his wife was expecting. His wife surprised him by having triplets. Now he's looking for two other men.

It was a very hot day in summer. The boss of an Irish house-painting crew went to check on his men. One of the men was dripping in sweat, wearing two jackets.

"What the hell have you got those two jackets on for?" asked the boss.

"And doesn't it say on the paint tin here 'Put on two coats'," replied the painter.

A disheveled, unshaven man walked into a hairdresser's and asked for a shave. The nervous Irish hairdresser managed to cut him three times while he was giving him a shave.

"Give me a razor," said the man.

"What do you want that for?" demanded the hairdresser. "Do you want to shave yourself?"

"No. I want to defend myself," said the man.

"I never have to worry about my wife going off with other men," bragged Danny. "She a wonderful, kind, considerate woman—not to mention—ugly."

Patrick went to see the parish priest.

"Father," he said, "before I die I'd like to convert to Protestantism."

"Why would you want to do a terrible thing like that?" asked the astonished priest.

"Well, surely you don't want to lose a good Catholic when I die, do you?" said Patrick.

Did you hear about the Irish lass who believed in long engagements?

She was pregnant six months before she got married.

Then there was the newly-married Irish girl who wrote to the army for all her husband's favourite recipes.

Then there was the Irish farmer who added iron pills as a supplement to his sheep's diet so he would get steel wool.

Did you hear about the Irish ventriloquist who started badly and found that attendance at his performances went from bad to worse?

His dummy left him.

A tourist driving in rural Ireland came to a ford in the road. (A ford in the road is where the stream normally trickles under the road and is expected to be swollen during the winter and cover the road surface).

The tourist saw a farmer and called out, "I say, is the water deep around here?"

The farmer said, "No, sir."

The motorist drove into the ford. The water came up and started coming in at the bottom of the driver's door. The water continues to come in until it started coming in through the driver's window.

The driver shouted out of the open window. "I thought you said the water wasn't deep here."

The farmer shouted back, "It only comes up to the waist of the ducks."

Pat, dressed in a suit, was talking to farmer Mick over a pint of Guinness.

"Mick," he said. "I'm starting a new business venture."

"Ah, you're a real entry-pre-new-ur Pat," replied the farmer. "If you don't mind me askin'," he continued, "What would it be?"

Mick puffed out his chest. "I've opened a launderette next to the local church."

"Have ya Pat?" said Mick, "Now why would ya be doin' dat?"

"Because Mick," said Pat. "Cleanliness is next to godliness."

Paddy had driven an old truck that was costing him more and more to maintain. He had saved for years to put down a deposit on a new Mack truck he had his eye on. The local dealer agreed to Paddy taking the top-of-the-line Mack for a test drive.

Paddy drove it off a cliff to test the air brakes.

Declan was living far from home in a small town near the Colorado mountains. One day he found a little bird with an injured wing in a ditch. He looked all around but couldn't see a nest or any other birds nearby. He took the baby bird home to care for it until it was strong enough to be released. The fledgling ate the food he gave it and grew. It gained in strength and was soon flapping its wings normally like it wanted to fly. Declan fed the bird morning and night and the bird ate everything put in front of it, so much so, that it grew noticeably. As it grew Declan realised that he didn't recognize what type if bird it was. Nobody else could recognize what species it was either. So Declan decided to call this rare species Rarey. The bird sat around all day eating until it was the size of a large cat. There was one problem though, it never attempted to fly. It demanded so much food that Declan couldn't afford to keep it. He had to figure out some way to make his feathered friend fly. He figured it was way past time for the bird to be released back into the wild. He had an inspiration. He would take the bird to the top of a high cliff and push it off. He had heard of mothers doing that to their chicks. He reasoned that the bird would instinctively flap its wings and soar like an eagle.

Once it was able to fly, Declan knew it would be able to use its formidable size to fend for itself. He carried the gigantic bird out to his Plymouth sedan and manager to squeeze it into the back seat. He drove up into the mountains above Colorado and up to edge of a cliff. With a great deal of puffing and blowing Declan carried the huge creature to the edge of the precipice ready to launch it.

Just as he was about to heave the bird off the edge, it turned to him, opened its beak and chirped, "It's a long way to tip a Rarey."

Shamus and Michael were taking about their friends.

"And where is Sean Kelly," said Michael, "it's been a long time since I've seen him around."

"Oh, he's left Ireland," said Shamus. "It was mystical."

"I didn't know that," said Michael. "Why did he go?"

"It was a sign," replied Shamus. "He happened to be driving through the countryside one day and he saw a sign that said 'Drink Canada Dry', and that's where he's gone."

There was an Irishman playing bingo. He had his bingo card and was sitting in the middle of some players. At one point the Irishman noticed that the man next to him had a particular number on his card when it was called.

"Hey! There it is. You've got that one," Damon called.

"Huh, oh yes," responded the player.

A few numbers later the Irishman again volunteered. "Oh look. You've got that one too."

The man next to the Irishman was getting a little upset by now. "I can damn well see I've got the number. Why can't you leave me alone," he said.

"Now I can't do that," said the Irishman, "mine filled up a while ago."

Two Irishmen were out on a country road on a tandem bicycle, Paddy in the front and Sean on the back. Having ridden up a very long and steep hill Paddy puffs, "I'll ha . . . have to stop for a . . . rest. I'm exhausted."

After a short rest Paddy said, "Begorrah, that hill was hard Sean. We only just made it to the top."

"Yes," agreed Sean, "And I'm sure we would have rolled backwards if I hadn't kept the brake on."

There was an Irishman who drove his car into the sea.

He wanted to dip his headlights.

Two Irishmen had been holidaying in Amsterdam for a week and went out to a local bordello. One slapped 1000 euros down on the reception desk and demanded, "Give me the stupidest looking girl you've got."

"But sir," said the woman, "for that money you can have the best and most beautiful woman we've got."

"Don't you worry about that," said the Irishman, "she's not for me. She's for him. He's homesick."

For a long time, Scotsmen and Irishmen had argued over the relative merits of Scotch and Irish whiskey. It had never been proven which of the two was better. Then an Irish farmer and his Scottish friend decided they would get an independent test performed to decide the matter once and for all.

The two men procured a bottle each of their respective national products.

Under controlled conditions in front of an auditor, the two men set to work removing labels and ensuring that there were no identifying marks on the bottles. Under the watchful eye of the auditor the men labeled one bottle "A", and the other bottle "B". Satisfied that all had been done properly, the auditor packaged the two bottles carefully and sent them off to the lab for analysis.

In due course, the results arrived and the men got together. The auditor opened the envelope, and read out the result.

"To whom it may concern: Regarding samples submitted for testing for analysis. Both samples have been through extensive testing which has now been completed. We must inform you that both horse "A" and horse "B" have the same strain of hepatitis."

An Irish business venture never got off the ground.

Its name was "Irish Glider Engines Inc."

An Irishman at work one day was asked by his boss to go out and buy him a pack of Winfield cigarettes. Within thirty minutes he returned from the shop empty-handed and told him that they didn't have any Winfield.

"In that case," the boss told him, "get anything they have got."

The Irishman left and returned thirty minutes later. He presented his boss with a pie.

Pat was on Grafton Street trying to find someone who could light his cigarette for him. He approached Sean.

"Got a light friend?" Pat asked.

"To be sure I do," replied Sean. He dug in his pockets. "I have a match here someplace."

He struck the match against a nearby window. Strike. Strike. Strike.

"I can't understand it," said Sean. Strike. Strike. Still no result. "It worked this morning."

Assume there is a small table in the middle of a huge square room. On the table is $1000 cash. There are three corners occupied, one vacant. In one corner is Father Christmas, in another the Easter Bunny and in another a smart Irishman. If they all ran to the cash at exactly the same time, which would get there first?

None of them. There's no such thing as Father Christmas, the Easter Bunny or a smart Irishman.

Two Irishmen who owned a hotel in County Mayo were discussing their financial problems. They were getting very few customers drinking at the hotel and even less staying in their accommodation. They were thinking they might have to go bankrupt.

"You know Declan," said Johnny, "We would make more money if we turned this place into a brothel."

"B . . . b . . .b . . . Broth-el," stammered Declan, "If we can't get them to drink beer and Guinness, how are we going to get them to drink broth?"

An Irishman returned to his home town after a long absence. He recognized a face across the street and went over to talk to him.

"To be sure, it's been a long time since I've seen you," said the Irishman. "But tell me now," he continued, "was it you or your brother who was killed in the war?"

THE IRISH JOKE BOOK

A man had to break the news to a woman that her husband had drowned in a vat of whiskey at the distillery.

After her initial shock and some tears, she managed to say something. "Thank you for coming to tell me," she said. "It must've been a terrible end."

"Oh now, it wasn't quite as bad as all that," said the man. "He came out a good few times to get something to eat."

Aidan was wandering through a zoo. He saw a forlorn-looking gorilla looking back at him from inside his cage. The Irishman went up to the cage and read the plaque.

It said, "Gorilla Missing Link Mating Experiment. For more information contact Zoological Genetic Husbandry Research at the Office."

Feeling concerned at how sad the gorilla looked, Aidan walked to the Zoo Office to ask. A man in a white lab coat answered the bell.

"Well, the gorilla you saw in the cage is a female," the male technician said." Unfortunately, her mate died and we cannot get another male gorilla."

"Oh, dat's so sad. I see now dat she is sad because she misses her mate," said Aidan.

"Indeed," said the technician. "Our research has therefore taken a new direction. We are looking into the theory that there is a missing link."

"I've heard of dat," said Aidan. "The theory dat we are descended from apes."

"Exactly," said the technician, "so the experiment now involves a search for suitable male homo sapiens to mate with our female gorilla."

The technician could see the realization that they were looking for a human male to mate with the gorilla come across Aidan's face.

"Incidentally there is $500 involved for the person willing to take part. Would you be willing to help us in this experiment?" asked the technician.

"I'll have to think about it," said Aidan as he left.

Next day he returned. "I've decided to take part in this experiment," said Aidan, "but only on three conditions. One—There's no kissing involved. Two—That if there is any resultant offspring, dat it's not named after me. And three—dat you allow me to pay the $500 off in installments."

Three men of the cloth were attending a religious unity conference in Scotland. In the middle of the conference a team-building exercise found the clergymen fully equipped with lifejackets, rods and fishing tackle to go fishing together. They stood together on the shore of the loch looking out over the calm waters. Having rowed out into the loch they weighed anchor a little way from shore.

The Scots minister, the English dean and the Irish priest chatted about the Bible story of Jesus and St. Peter, and how they themselves were fishers of men. The Scots minister's line became fouled and having no more of that particular tackle available, he decided he'd like to go ashore and get some more. He got down on his knees and prayed earnestly, then stepped over the side of the boat and walked on the surface of the water to the shore, returning the same way.

After a while the English dean needed to go ashore and he also knelt down and prayed. He also stepped over the side of the boat and walked on the surface of the water to the shore, returning the same way.

After another couple of hours, the clergymen found that their food was running low. Realizing that it was his turn, the Irish priest said that he would go, so he got down on his knees and prayed. He then stepped over the side of the boat and promptly sank into the water.

The minister turned to the dean and said, "Och, for the sake of unity, perhaps we should have pointed out where the stepping stones were."

An Irish marketing executive regularly flew to various destinations in Europe for weeks on end. Back early one evening, the phone rang and he answered it briefly and then hung up.

"Who was that dear?" called his wife from the other end of the house.

"Oh," he replied, "a wrong number. Some ejit asked if the coast was clear. I told him dis was not de weather service."

An Irishman approached the pearly gates. St. Peter was there to greet him.

"What is your name, my son?" asked St. Peter.

"Patrick Flannigan," replied the Irishman.

St. Peter turned the pages of the large book and said, "Oh yes, here you are. You may go in."

"You must be bored with your job of showing people in to heaven year after year," said the Irishman.

"You must remember time operates on a different scale here in heaven," said St. Peter. "A million years are but as one minute, a million dollars are but as one cent."

"That's interesting," said Patrick, "would you let me borrow a cent, your eminence?"

"Certainly Mr. Flannigan," said St. Peter, "If you would just wait a minute."

Did you hear about the Irishman whose car was painted green on one side, and red on the other?

He loved to hear witnesses contradict each other.

An old man was propping up the bar at a high-class Dublin wedding. A man in a suit approached the bar to order a drink.

"Excuuse me shir," slurred the old man, "are you de bridegroom?"

"No sir," replied the Irishman, "I was eliminated in the semi-finals."

An Irishman seated himself at a restaurant and the waiter moved to his table.

"Will you have a red wine or a white wine with your dinner," the waiter asked the Irishman.

"It doesn't matter much to me," said the Irishman, "I'm colorblind."

One night an Irishman was riding a bicycle around the center of Dublin without lights. A policeman on his beat saw this and called out to him to stop.

"What's your name," demanded the policeman, as he pulled a notebook and pencil from his pocket.

"John Smith," answered the cyclist.

"That can't be your name," said the policeman as licked the pencil, "will you ever be telling me your real name."

"Me name is William," said the Irishman slowly, "William Shakespeare."

"Dere," said the policeman, "Dat wasn't dat hard was it?"

An Irish worker went into the office to see his boss to ask for some time off.

THE IRISH JOKE BOOK

"But you've already had time off for your mother-in-law's funeral, your daughter's measles, your son's Holy Communion. What is it now?" asked the boss.

"I'm getting married, sir", said the Irishman.

Did you hear about the Irish woman who fell overboard into the shark-infested waters of the Irish Sea?

The sharks didn't touch her because they were man-eaters.

There was an Irishman who snored so loud that he'd often wake himself up. He cured himself. He now sleeps in the next room.

It is easy to recognize an Irishman on an oil rig.

He's the one throwing bread up to the helicopters.

Two Irishman, one in Dublin and the other in Galway, were sentenced to a term of imprisonment on the same day and found they were sharing a cell. They were pleased to see that they had separate single beds, rather than bunk beds.

"How long would you be in for?" one of them asked the other.

"Eight years," said the other.

"You'll be out before me den," said the other, "I've got ten years. So you'd better take the bed by the door."

A Texan was sitting in a bar in Dublin and as he got drunker he got louder and louder. He started boasting about his state.

"In Texas, a man can get on a train on Monday morning, eat and sleep on the train all through Monday, Tuesday, and when he gets off the train on Wednesday, he's still in Texas."

The dour Irishman beside him turns to him and says, "You have me sympathy stranger. In Ireland we have slow trains like dat too."

An Irishman rushed into a police station and told the duty sergeant that his car had just been stolen.

"Did you get a look at the thief?" asked the sergeant.

"No," said the Irishman, "but I got his number."

An Irishman had been at the pub for quite some time. At closing time he got a hip bottle of whiskey, shoved it in his back pocket and staggered home. On the way however, at one point he fell backwards and broke the flask of whiskey—the broken glass causing lacerations to one arse cheek. Thankfully the whiskey sterilized the wounds. When he finally got home, he removed his trousers and set about the task of trying to cover the cuts with sticking plaster.

He couldn't see what he was doing, and had the bright idea of using the dressing table mirror to help him and so with the plastering job finished, he went off to bed. Careful not to wake his wife, he eased in on his side, suppressing his desire to cry out in pain and fell asleep.

Next morning, his wife got up to get breakfast. She returned to the bedroom and shook him awake.

"You were drunk when you got home last night weren't you?" she said.

"No-o. No-o. I was nottt," he said.

"Yes you was. I know you was. You lazy, good-for-nuthin' piece of shite," she said.

"But dear," replied the husband, "what makes you think dat about me?"

"I can tell from all of the sticking plasters stuck on the mirror," she said.

There was an Irishman who smoked and drank and became very unfit. With his lifestyle compounded with an aversion to exercise, he also became very lazy. Hoping he might change with an independent opinion, his wife forced him to go to the doctor for a checkup.

The doctor advised he completely change his lifestyle—give up his bad habits, get outdoors and get some exercise.

"I suggest that you try some walking. Start with walking a mile in a day, the next day two miles, the next day three. Walk an extra mile each day. Do you understand?"

"I think so doctor," said the Irishman.

"So how many miles would you walk on the fourth day then?" asked the doctor.

"Four miles," replied the man.

"And how many on the fifth day?"

"Five," the Irishman answered.

"Good man," said the doctor, "You've got it. I'm confident with that advice you'll start to regain your fitness."

"Tanks a lot doc," said the Irishman.

"No trouble," said the doctor, "Anyway come back to me in a couple of weeks for further advice."

The Irishman phoned the doctor two weeks later. "Your advice was wonderful doc," he said, "I feel so much fitter now."

"That's good," said the doctor.

"But," said the Irishman, "my wife is still mad with me."

"That's bad," said the doctor. "Come in to see me so I can give you a full examination."

"I will be able to in a while doc," said the man, "but right now I'm about a hundred miles away."

"Why are you working so late Declan?" asked the boss.

"And don't I always start at eight o'clock," replied Declan.

"But that should be a.m., not p.m.," advised the boss.

"Ah so," said Declan, "I was wondering why my wife gives me a roast meal for breakfast."

In a public bar in Dublin, a man has a dog on a lead. The dog cannot wait any longer and does his business on the floor. The man and the dog leave.

Within a minute Sean comes into the pub. On his way to the bar, he steps on the dog's business, slips over and falls heavily.

As he is picking himself up, Pat comes in and he too skids in the dog's mess, bangs his elbow in the fall.

"Ooh, me elbow," groans Pat.

"And I did that a moment ago," said Sean.

With that Pat got up quickly, punches Pat and yells, "Filthy beast."

A senior hospital specialist is talking to a medical student in a hospital training room. He holds up a part of a human body.

"And what is this," he asks.

"It's a kneecap," answers the medical student.

"Mother of God, no," says the specialist, "'tis a brain I'm holding."

He puts it down and lifts up something else.

"And what am I holding now," he asks.

"I tink it's a bedpan," replies the student.

"Holy Mary, St. Joseph and sweet baby Jesus, no. Not at all. It's a human skull." says the specialist becoming increasingly exasperated.

The specialist hoists up another bone.

"Can you tell me what human bone I'm holding up now?"

"Now, dat'd be a rib," says the student.

"Mother of God man," says the specialist. "This is a thigh bone. This is astounding. After all of this time you have been training to become a doctor, you obviously know nothing. Not a single solitary ting. How are you going to pass you final exam?"

"But I didn't think the final exam was until tomorrow," says the student.

"I heard this funny joke the other day," says O'Shea to Murphy. "I'll try you out with it. I'll ask you a question, and you try to answer it."

"Okay," said Murphy, "I try."

Let me see now . . . how did it go? Ah yes. How do you get down from an elephant?" asked O'Shea.

"Mm. I know," said Murphy, "you get the elephant to walk and stop beside a ladder, and you get down on the ladder."

"No," said O'Shea.

"Ah yes, you would slide down the elephant's trunk," ventured Murphy.

"No," said O'Shea.

"Well now," said Murphy, "you would grab the tail and swing down off dat."

"No," said O'Shea.

"Well den," said Murphy, "I give up. How do you get down from an elephant?"

"Ha ha. I've got you dis time," gloated O'Shea. "You don't, you get down from a goose."

"That's good," said Murphy, and then he paused. "But how do you get down from a goose."

"I'm not dat sure," said O'Shea, "but I think it's because it's not nearly as tall as an elephant."

Don, limping home, came across his old friend Jerry.

"Jesus, Mary and holy St. Joseph," exclaimed Jerry, "would ya look at you with yer bloody nose, yer black eye and yer torn coat. What happened Don?"

"I got into a fight with Dan O'Duggin," said Don.

"You mean that objectionable little runt I see in the pub sometimes," said Jerry. "How in the name of Jesus, Mary and holy St. Joseph did that argumentative little pip-squeak do dat to you?"

"Now Jerry," said Don, "I'll not have you speaking ill of the dead."

How do you make ninety-nine lumps on an Irishman's head?

Hang him using bungee rope."

"How did your nose get so red, Michael?" a friend asked.

"It got banged," replied Michael.

"How did you get that red nose, Michael?" another friend asked.

"I went and banged it," replied Michael.

"Did you know, Michael, yer nose if lookin' very red," confided another friend.

"Ah now, I did know dat," replied Michael.

"And how would you be doint dat den," continued the friend.

"I bit it," replied Michael.

"And how was it dat you were able to do dat?" he asked.

"Easy. I just climbed up on a chair, and there it was," said Michael.

An Irishman coming home from the pub was trying to be quiet so that he didn't disturb his wife. On the way along the hall to the stairs, he tripped on a rug upsetting a table with a vase full of flowers on it.

From upstairs his wife shouted, "What was that? What are you doing down there?"

"Itsh all-right dear," he called out, I was jusht walking through the lounge when the goldfish attacked me."

An Irishman wishing to join the Returned Servicemen's League was being interviewed by the committee.

"So you wish to join the RSL?" asked one.

"Dat I do," said the Irishman.

"So do you have a war record," asked another.

"Indeed I do," the Irishman replied. "I have Vera Lynn's White Cliffs of Dover."

"And what is that mark on your face?" asked Patrick.

"Oh, that's just a birthmark," replied Michael.

"Ah so. So how long have you had that?"

An unemployed Irishman went to the dole office to look for a job. His wife was with him.

He was told that the only position available was a job as a diver. If he made his way down to the pier and asked to speak to the head diver, he would be the first one to go for the position.

Off they went. There was no-one at the land-end of the pier, but they could see figures at the sea-end of the pier. After the long walk, they asked a man who told them, "He's down there." The man pointed to where a thick tube went over the steps down into the water.

The Irishman began removing his clothes. He was down to his underwear. Just before he jumped into the water, he turned to his wife and said, "If I don't come back, you'll know I've got the job."

An Irishwoman on holiday pulled the hotel notepaper out of the drawer in the hotel room to write a letter to her son.

"Dear Michael," she wrote, "I just want you to know I am having a good time and will be back home soon. Now Michael, I know how much trouble you have with your reading so I am writing this very slowly . . ."

An Irishman was at a wine tasting.

The wine salesman said, "See how you like this well-matured claret."

"Yes, that is nice," said the Irishman, "a good complement for baked potatoes."

"This superb vintage wine is twelve years old," said the salesman.

"I don't think I want to buy any of that," said the Irishman. "It hasn't been selling very well has it?"

"Would you like to come with me to see the hew Spice Girls movie, Sean?" asked Pat.

"Well I would," replied Sean, "but I don't think I can afford to go."

"Aw come on," said Pat, "it's supposed to be real good."

"No, I really can't," said Sean. "Anyhow, I can't get any holidays from work for a fair while, and I don't like flying in an airplane."

Two Irishmen were in a light aircraft. The engine started to splutter. When they decided to bail out, they realised there was only one parachute.

One of them put on the parachute and the other held his leg as they jumped out of the plane together. They decided to free-fall to get away from the aircraft that was spinning out of control nearby.

At 10,000 feet the Irishman without a parachute pulled the fake leg of the other Irishman and shouted out, "Hey, open the chute!"

"No. Plenty of time yet," shouted back the other.

At 5,000 feet another pull on the leg—"Hey, open the chute!"

"No. Still plenty of time," shouted back the other.

At 1,000 feet frantic pulling on the leg—"Hey, open the chute!"

"Don't panic! We've still got time left," shouted back the other.

At a rapid descent speed at 100 feet, the Irishman with the chute called down to his friend, "It really doesn't matter now. We can jump from here . . ."

A Boston Irishman had served in the US Army for some years. He was to be sent on a one-man mission, parachuting in behind enemy lines. The briefing officer explained to him that the drop site would be marked so that it was clearly visible from the air. Also there would be a jeep camouflaged somewhere nearby for his use.

The pilot told him the drop zone was in sight, so now was the time to jump. The Irishman jumped, and remembering his training on clearing the aircraft, counted to ten and pulled the ripcord.

But nothing happened.

He felt around for the emergency ripcord and gave that a firm pull.

Again, nothing happened.

He rolled his eyes and said to himself, "Typical rotten army preparation—and I bet the jeep won't be there either."

Did you hear about the Irish veterinarian?

He tried to separate Siamese cats.

An Irish priest on a trip to Israel was visiting the Sea of Galilee. He was horrified when told the outrageous price to be ferried across the sea by the ferryman.

As he stormed off, he was heard to be saying, "No wonder Jesus walked."

An Irish con-man went to New York, but he didn't have a great deal of luck. The first man that he tried to sell the Brooklyn Bridge to turned out to be owner. So the Irishman had to pay him $100 so the owner wouldn't tell the cops.

An Irishman on a building site was working at an incredibly fast rate. Every couple of minutes he would dash up the ladder with a back-breaking load of bricks. After seeing this go on for an hour, a friend asked him why he was working so hard.

"Aw," he said with a twinkle in his eye, "don't tell them but I've got them all fooled. I'm not really working that hard. It's the same load of bricks every time."

An eminent Irish archeologist was giving a lecture at the University of Southern California in a monotonous tone.

"Some of the cities of the past," he droned, "have vanished so completely that it's doubtful if some of them existed at all."

What is the definition of an Irish intellectual?

An Irishman who goes to a museum or an art gallery when it isn't raining.

How do you know you've got an Irishman in the car-wash?

He's sitting on a bicycle.

Two young lads from Galway on the west coast of Ireland took a trip all the way to Dublin on the east coast. While they were there they went to the cinema for the first time. The film had already started. In the darkness the usherette walked towards them up the aisle with a torch.

"Look out," said one lad to the other, "there's a bicycle up ahead."

An Irishman bought his wife a pair of rubber gloves.

When he asked her how she liked them, she said, "They're really very good. When I've got them on sure, I can wash my hands without getting them wet."

Did you hear about the Irishman who was given a pair of cuff links for his birthday?

Since he didn't have that kind of shirt, he had his wrists pierced.

An extremely unattractive Irishman claimed he had been beautiful as a baby but he had been exchanged by the gypsies.

An Irishman flew into John F Kennedy airport. He was stopped at Customs to have his two big black plastic bags inspected. Full of telephones, he was asked what they were for.

"I don't know," he said. "I've just got a job with a New Jersey jazz band. Didn't they ask me to bring two sacks of phones with me?"

Did you hear about the Irish kidnapper?

He enclosed a stamped-addressed envelope with the ransom demand.

An Irishman was in a casual clothing store. After trying on baseball caps for half an hour, he walked up to the shop assistant and said, "Do you have any with the peak at the back?"

An Irish detective was escorting a prisoner to the police station when a sudden gust of wind carried his hat away down the road.

"Shall I go off and get it for you," asked the prisoner.

"What do you take me for?" said the detective. "A fool? No. You wait here and I'll go and fetch it."

At the local drinking — Brendon Kelly 2012

Index

Aer Lingus
        Pilot with plane in trouble   11
        Catch home with domino   16
        Man wearing cowboy hat   39
        landing on the shortest runway   44

Alcohol
        And alcohol alone that is responsible   26

Alcoholic and the brain transplant   35

Arabs
        Why do Arabs have oil   15
        And the domino tournament   16

Australian
        Australians of Irish descent   17
        Scotsman wanted to change into an   22
        Brain valued at $1500 35

Baby
        Doctor was preparing to deliver the   31
        Bird home to care for it   51
        Beautiful as a   73

Bank
        Decide to rob a   14
        Bookie and accept a bank check   34

Bar

A man walks into a   15
And Michael O'Shea   22
Of soap   46
At a high-class Dublin wedding   60
Texan was sitting in a   62
A dog on a lead in a   64

Barn animals in the   32

Bartender (Barman)

And the great Irish jokes   15
And the green bullfrog   21
Poured the two pints   29

Beer

Written on the bottom of   7
Can't get them to drink   56

Bicycle

On a tandem bicycle   53
Riding without lights   60
in car-wash   72
in cinema   72

Bomb

In the boot   12
After an IRS bomb explosion   34
What do you get for throwing   47

Bordello in Amsterdam   54

Brothel   56

Bottle

On the bottom of Irish beer   7
Large enough for the stick   16
Of whiskey over my grave   27
I fetch the   41

Of Scotch and Irish whiskey   54
At closing time he got a hip   62

Brain

Surgeon and bum   12
Half a brain   13
Swallowing a fly18
Piece of paper and brain   18
Removing part of   22
Never been used   35
The rejuvenated brain   43
Brainwash an Irishman   48
Specialist holding a brain   65

Bus

Blow up a bus   9
Collecting fares on   12
Busload   46

Car

Parked   7
for its first service   13
Painted   59
Stolen   62
Car-wash   72

Church

doors   13
Next to the launderette   51

Cigarettes

Lighting with a match   55
Buying Winfield cigarettes   55

Coffin

With only two handles   17
The open coffin   29
And the piano   32

Court and accustomed places   24

Cuff links and wrists   73

Dead
　　　Business in the gutter   23
　　　And pouring a bottle   27
　　　Seagull   34
　　　Face-down   38
　　　Man and dragged him   41
　　　Amazed that he wasn't   45
　　　Found in a brick   67

Dip headlights   54

Dock
　　　Clambering to fit in the   24
　　　Offender in the   27

Doctor
　　　And burning his other ear   8
　　　Hole where armpit used to be   10
　　　Appendix transplant   21
　　　And toilet water   24
　　　And the light   31
　　　And the brain transplant   35
　　　And the walking   63
　　　And the bones   65

Dog
　　　Burying my   10
　　　Walking his   23
　　　A bionic   43
　　　In a public bar   64
　　　dogs and flat faces   7

Drink, drinking, drinks, drunk
　　　Drinks on the house   21
　　　Drink his presents   27

THE IRISH JOKE BOOK

Evils of drinking   28
Pub called last   32
The demon drink   32
And the stewardess   39
At the local drinking Guinness   40
Drink Canada Dry   53
Drink broth   54
And the semi-finals   60
Drunk and the shiny object in the sky   27
Drunker and boasting   62
Drunk and sticking plasters   62

Dublin

Not Dublin but Jerusalem   11
And the flat tire   15
And Michael O'Shea   22
And double-yellow lines   26
Two Texans in a Dublin pub   29
Hospital and expensive transplant   35
And Brown from   40
Transferred to Dublin branch   43
Talking in a Dublin pub   49
60, 61, 62, 64, 72

Ear

Burn an Irishman's   7
Burn his other   8

Easter

With a bag of Easter eggs   20
Bunny and in another a smart Irishman   56

Evil

Plans in mind   12
Evils of drinking   28

Farmer

Sean rang the doctor   31
And only room for two in the house   36

Holding a huge pile of manure   45
Who added iron pills   50
And water in the ford   51
And his Scottish friend decided   54

Farmhouse, light on at a   35

Foreman
And the nails won't go in the wood   21
And his hand questions at the job interview   36
And three questions at the job interview   38

Glider
Engines Inc.   55

Gorilla
Adopted an Irishman   30
Mating experiment   57

Grenade
In his mouth   8
Pulled the pin out of my hand   10

Guinness
And the clean glass   29
And the Irish martini   30
At the local drinking   40
Bottle of cold   41
Over a pint of   51
Get them to drink beer and   56

Hole
IQ and digs holes   7
Where his armpit should be   10
To bury my dog   14

Horse
Drowned four horses   10
Horses that he couldn't tell apart   16

THE IRISH JOKE BOOK

Not one could get a grip   22
Paid   1000 to   1 33
Holding the horse manure   45
And the strain of hepatitis   55

Hospital

With a large hole   10
And the brain transplant   35
Training room   65

House

To paint a   9
Building a new   21
Drinks were on the   21
Visited by a Cardinal   36
-painting crew   49
Wife from the other end of the   59

IRA bomb explosion   34

Indian

Forgot the name of that   29
Jew and Irishman   35

Intellectual, definition of   72

Jesus

Born in Jerusalem instead of Dublin   11
Was born in Bethlehem   38
And St. Peter   58
Sweet baby   65
Mary and holy St. Joseph   66
Walked on the Sea of Galilee   71

Jew

Called Di   29
Indian and Irishman   33

Ladder

Nine to turn the   9
Deep enough to fit the   14
Kicks away the   17
Different to an ordinary one   20
Elephant to stop beside a   66
Dash up the   72

Lake

Sloping   10
Rowed out to the center of the   42

Lawyer was representing   25

London

To blow up a bus   9
Expecting to find it paved with gold   15
And you meet an Englishman   40
A multi-national company in   42
Advised him to fly into   48

Married

Pregnant six months before she got   50
And needing time off   61

Money

$1000 cash   56

Oil

Why do the Arabs have   15
Recognize an Irishman on an oil rig   61

Paint

How many to paint a house   9
Bunnies on his head   20
House-painting crew   49
Painted green on one side   59

THE IRISH JOKE BOOK

Parachute

    The new Irish   21
    First jump after completing training   28
    Only one   70

Party

    On the roof   21
    And help him drink his presents   27

Phone

    Him while he is ironing   7
    Ring the doctor   8
    The company head office in New York   43
    Rang and he answered it briefly   59
    Phoned the doctor two weeks later   64
    two sacks of phones   73

Pig

    Spoke up and said   11
    In the barn   36
    Irishman who marries a   46

Pilot

    With plane in trouble   11
    And his co-pilot   44
    Irish kamikaze pilots   47
    Told him the drop zone was in sight   71

Plane

    Why don't Irish fly planes? 11
    In trouble radios   11
    And missed the Earth   12
    Leveled out at   10,000 feet   29
    To a screaming halt   44
    Don't like flying in an airplane   70
    Jumped out of the plane together   70

Playing bingo   53

Playing Spot the Ball   25

Potato
    And four-course meal   9
    Why do the Irish have potatoes? 15
    Into a pint of Guinness   30
    Good complement for baked potatoes   69

Pregnant
    23
    50

Priest
    glowered down over the congregation   32
    was giving his parishioners his usual sermon   40
    Patrick went to see the parish   50
    The Scots minister, the English dean and the Irish   58
    On a trip to Israel   71
    And the Scots minister and the English dean   58

Protestant
    Protestants per gallon   47
    I'm a Protestant   49
    Convert to Protestantism   50

Pub
    With a bomb in the back   12
    Pass the parcel in an Irish   20
    An Irishman walked into a   21
    Two Texans walked into a Dublin   29
    Called last drinks   32
    Just after an IRA   34
    Irishmen were talking in a Dublin   43
    For quite some time   62
    Bar in Dublin, a man has a dog on a lead   64
    Objectionable little runt I see in the   67
    Was trying to be quiet   68

THE IRISH JOKE BOOK

Record
>White Cliffs of Dover   68

Scotland, Scotsman, Scotsmen
>A Scotsman wanted to have an operation   22
>For a long time Scotsmen and Irishmen 54

A religious unity conference in   58

Sex
>maniac   49
>on the TV   24

Space, Spaceship   13, 16, 30, 42

St. Peter at the pearly gates   59

Submarine   8, 19, 26

Surgeon   12, 22

Telephone
>And the wrong number   24

Tip a Rarey   52

Warehouse   41,

Washing
>In rubber gloves   73

Whiskey   27, 40, 62
>relative merits of Scotch and Irish whiskey   54
>drowning in a vat of   57

Wife
>I thought it was my   27
>His wife's waters had broke   31
>Asked him what sort of gravestone   39

What did the Irishman say to his   46
Wife-beating Methods   47
Was expecting   49
Going off with other men   50
From the other end of the house   59
Careful not to wake his   62
Forced him to go to the doctor for a checkup   63
Gives me a roast meal for breakfast   64
So that he didn't disturb his   68
His wife was with him   68
A pair of rubber gloves   73

Window
Jumping out of basement windows   13
On the bottom floors of Irish apartment buildings   14
Windows to keep the fish out   19
She fell out the   23
Hanging up in the   33
Count the number of basement windows   47
Through the driver's   51
He struck the match against a nearby   56

Printed in Great Britain
by Amazon.co.uk, Ltd.,
Marston Gate.